The Left-Handed Drummer

I0153537

Tips for Drummers and Drum Instructors

Thomas P. Bittner

Copyright © 2018 Thomas P. Bittner

ISBN: 978-3-00-060170-5

IMPRINT

Published by Amazon Self-Publishing, 2018
First published in Germany, 2017 in German
Print: Amazon, print on demand
Cover Design: Thomas Bittner
Cover Photo: Thomas Bittner
Portrait-Foto: © Jürgen Olczyk München (Jat Photo Intern. Jürgen Olczyk) for drummer's focus, with friendly permission
Translation from German: Elizabeth Lamberts
Layout: Thomas Bittner
Thomas Bittner asserts the moral right to be identified as the author of this work

Author: Thomas Bittner
Erdinger Str. 3
D-85447 Fraunberg
Germany

PREFACE

This isn't a scientific book. By no means do I claim it's either complete or completely correct; I didn't forget to cite sources, I left them out intentionally. Please take this book as a reflection of my own experiences with left-handed drumming; playing as well as instructing others.

My goal in writing this is to shed some light on aspects which most people I've discussed this topic with simply aren't aware of. Thanks to their interest and encouragement, I've taken up the challenge to collect what I've learned, recording it in the form of this book you now hold in your hands.

I hope this book inspires you, my readers, to give more thought to left-handed drumming. Please approach this topic with an open mind, and dare to question your own beliefs and premises. Hopefully this book will awaken your curiosity and launch you on your own search for more information on the subject – especially if you feel personally affected. After all, in this internet day and age research has become astonishingly easy and the pool of information at our fingertips virtually endless.

By directly addressing the reader I hope to engage with you – especially you lefties – on a personal level.

CONTENTS

INTRODUCTION

Let me guess: You're either a lefty yourself and have chosen probably the only instrument you can convert from right to left-handed: The drum set. Or you're a drum teacher working with lefties, and have come to realize there must be a valid reason your students should switch their drum setup from right-handed to left-handed.

To help you understand why this is so important, please let me start by telling you my story as a drummer. My own musical journey wasn't the easiest; at times it was a path of suffering. It took me a long time to reach the point where I was ready to bite the bullet re-learn: After having played drums the "wrong way around" for almost 20 years, I decided to switch my setup from right-handed to left-handed. Honestly, at the beginning it didn't feel like re-learning, but like starting all over again.

But from that moment on, everything changed. Suddenly things just took off, and my progress on the drum set eclipsed anything I'd experienced prior. The decision to start all over again, my progress during the years and all the ups and downs I had to go through have inspired me to collect my thoughts and advice in the form of this book, which I'm excited to share with you. I hope this may help others facing the struggles of being a left-handed drummer to take the plunge and dare to start over. The hardest part is learning to look not only at drumming, but at your entire world with fresh eyes…

It used to drive me nuts when my drum teacher told me to "practice more" – especially when I was already practicing hours a day! But now I see why: My progress was creeping along at a snail's pace. Back then, though, I had nothing to compare it to. It was only after I re-built my set left-handed that I experienced how quickly your body can learn, and how easy everything can be. And when I say everything, I don't just mean drumming!

People around me could sense my transition: I became more relaxed and, basically, more fun to be around. This new feeling of lightness helped me stop fighting; I no longer had to prove myself to anyone. I discovered that some things develop their own sense of momentum and don't need me to set them in motion or keep them going. I could finally stop working so damned hard and let things go with the flow – and still be successful.

This change in my personality has positively impacted my work as a drum teacher, too. Students who I once found difficult and demanding became sociable and pleasant to be around. One thing I'll never forget: A fellow teacher asked me to take over one of his students, whom he was at a loss to teach any further. Their lessons had become exhausting, the atmosphere between them was awkward and uncomfortable. To put it bluntly, he was at the end of his rope! And this coming from a teacher I admire for being patient, professional and strong. I accepted the challenge and helped his student through the process of switching from wrong-handed to left-handed drumming. Within a year he had made significant progress – blossoming into a great drummer with strong groove and expression.

One day he opened up to me, thanking me for the role I'd played in helping him undergo a meaningful change in his life. His friends noticed how much more relaxed he'd become, more fun to be around. Studying had also become easier – not only had his drum skills improved, but his grades had too! It seemed his life in general had become less of a struggle and more enjoyable.

You can imagine my goosebumps; it was as if I was listening to him tell my own story from just a few years earlier! It was a fantastic confirmation of my theory; and it wasn't to be the last such experience, either.

When you set out to learn playing the drums, the first thing you learn is a series of beats alternating between your right and left hands. At this point you're not really focused on how your drum set is arranged. A right-handed person will likely start the series with their right hand, whereas a lefty will probably start with their left. This is the first critical stage for an instructor: Those in tune with their students should recognize which hand they naturally begin with, classify their students as natural righties or lefties and teach them accordingly. Those who tend to cruise through these first lessons on auto-pilot, though, may overlook this critical juncture and teach a left-handed student to play right-handed. And just like that, a lefty is damned to what will probably be a long path of suffering at the drum set.

You may wonder why it's so important to adapt your beat pattern to your natural disposition. I firmly believe this is the only way you can tap into your inherent flow, allowing you to execute basic movements with ease. This sets the stage for what I call "flow", the fascination which gets you hooked on drumming for life!

It may sound contradictory, but for me this core of serenity releases an awesome energy, often called "groove". When your audience senses this energy you feel it in their response – it's the "special sauce" that can turn a simple gig into a legendary experience. And it's not only the audience who feels it, but your fellow band members also pick up on this energy and experience your jamming in a more intense way. Ironically, the drummer may be the last to notice the impact of this energy on their surroundings – it's a subtle process.

"Groove" isn't something you can conjure at will, nor something you can control. But a seasoned drummer can, with experience, build up their personal repertoire of patterns to help "get into the groove". Imagine what it must be like for a drummer who can't tap into this natural flow, but is instead locked into a set of patterns that contradicts their instinct… it's like driving with the handbrake on.

You see, when we try to force ourselves to do something with ease it usually just doesn't work. We end up trying too hard, and that effort ends up killing the very effortlessness we seek.

I think it all comes down to the fundamental balance between the two poles *action* and *letting go*, which we can also refer to as *active* and *passive*. I recently found an awesome quote – "The opposite of action isn't inaction, it's presence". For me, that sums up our elementary struggle between taking action and letting go, or going with the flow. These poles aren't necessarily opposites, and I wouldn't argue that one is better than the other. Instead, each relies on the other to exist.

Ironically, achieving the sense of ease I've described above can be the most exhausting thing in the world! *Letting go* is a real challenge for most of us. We end up trying too hard and putting in way too much effort, which in turn blocks us from achieving the very effortlessness we seek.

How often have you asked someone how they did something really amazing and they answered "I don't know... I didn't do anything... it just happened!" This "not doing anything" is the manifestation of *passiveness*. Of course they did something – otherwise nothing would have happened, right? They *took action* – but in doing so, they paradoxically *let go*; they allowed their action to develop so naturally that whatever awesome thing they achieved felt as if it happened on its own.

For me, the key is finding a balance between the poles *action* and *letting go*, or *active* and *passive*. In our Western culture, though, *active* is definitely the dominant of the two!

Over the years I have met many drummers who were so focused on forcing something to happen, they didn't realize they were actually standing in the way of allowing that very thing to happen. Their intense focus on controlling every element of their play threw most of their weight on the side of *action*, leaving no room for *letting go*. Drummers who never let themselves be *passive* will, I fear, never be able to find that crucial balance between these two essential poles.

Our Western culture frowns upon *passiveness* as being akin to "laziness" – and just plain unacceptable! I'm probably not the only one who will argue that it's healthy to be lazy once in a while. Those who haven't let go and been *passive*, as well as taken control and been *active* won't be able to strike a healthy balance.

For this reason, I truly hope to inspire my students to embrace good old-fashioned laziness. It's no big deal if they don't have time to practice once in a while – they shouldn't stress out about it. If they feel constantly under pressure to practice they often end up forcing themselves to practice when they feel they must, rather than choosing to practice when they feel motivated to. This is a fine line we instructors should tread with care – too much "laziness" can lead to too little practicing, which in turn will keep our students from making real progress on their instruments.

Our goal should be to help them accept their "lazy phases": If you really don't feel like practicing, then don't. Practicing when you are focused and concentrated – in other words, when you are in the mood to practice – is the most effective way to learn an instrument.

One of the most meaningful experiences I've gained from learning to play an instrument is developing my own sense of balance between being *active* and being *passive*. The first time I was truly aware of the power of *letting go* was at my drum set, as I experienced first-hand what amazing things can develop when you ease up on the *action* and let yourself *go with the flow*. Since then, this principle has enriched many other aspects of my personal and professional life.

One of the first places we can discover these natural poles *active* and *passive* is in our own bodies – in the form of right and left. But this is just one in a long line of characteristics used to differentiate between right and left – I'll dive deeper into this a bit later.

In the chapter "Our two brain hemispheres" I'll take a shot at making this natural polarization more tangible; first using logical explanations, then describing how we perceive it – the feeling we get in our own bodies.

1. CHALLENGES OF BEING A LEFTY

Let's start with the obvious: Lefties do everything with their left hand, just like righties do everything with their right hand. So far, so good?

Unfortunately, it's not as simple as that. For a lefty, the left side of their body is the active side – the one you do things with. We brush our teeth with our left hand, kick a ball with our left foot… the list of things we do with the left hand side of our bodies is virtually endless.

And, no big surprise here, righties do all the same things with the right hand / foot / side of their bodies.

We shouldn't lose sight of one important factor: We live in a world dominated by, therefore optimized for right-handed people. Growing up, a left-handed child is consistently confronted with things not designed for them. People who grow up right-handed usually don't notice their struggles because for them, the same experiences just "fit".

It's only natural that most lefties are – when compared to righties – very flexible with their "other" hand. Some natural lefties – after years of experience making things fit and learning to do things with their "passive" right hand – may not even realize they're left-handed!

Other lefties have simply accepted their fate, and live with the fact that cutting with scissors hurts, can openers don't work, swinging a scythe doesn't yield results and using a soup ladle is guaranteed to end with a mess. How could it not, with the spout on the wrong side? But don't worry, I won't roll out endless lists of examples; you lefties know this already, and I don't want to bore my right-handed readers…

The point I'd like to make here is that although these constant, unconscious adjustments can help lefties unlock creativity, they are also a hinderance in daily life. Some of us learn to adapt while preserving our left-handedness, but others adapt to the point of losing touch with their natural disposition.

Here's some fun trivia:
Did you know that the world's first modern left-handed concert grand piano was introduced by Blüthner pianos at the Frankfurt Music Fair in 2001? Company head Christian Blüthner is a lefty, as is his father.

But that's not all! Did you know that there are even people working on special sheet music for left-handed musicians? The theory goes that when their hands move from right to left, their eyes shouldn't have to move in the opposite direction – from left to right. This is why lefties tire more quickly when reading large amounts of text (such as a book); the effort this puts on their eyes and brain can be exhausting.

Growing up, a left-handed child doesn't realize that most tools are created to be used with a (dominant) right hand. They quickly learn to adapt themselves to each new situation as they deal with the obstacles daily life throws at them. Interestingly, left-handed children resort to using their "passive" hand much more often than their right-handed counterparts and usually end up using both hands almost equally as often. This helps them develop a high degree of creativity, improvisation and flexibility. But on the flipside, this leaves the door open for self-denial to creep in. I have noticed a fair amount of absent-mindedness in my work with left-handed children.

Let me give you an example. One of my friends has a child who, for me, is clearly a lefty. His father doesn't seem to be avoiding the issue – and says his son simply prefers to do some things with his right hand and other things with his left. His rationale is that his son doesn't display any clear signs of left-handedness. This argument sets my alarm bells ringing, proving the point in the other direction! I saw his son just a few days ago, and watched as he played with a dull children's knife. He held the knife in his left hand while trying to slide it into its leather sheath. The blade just wouldn't fit into the sheath, which he held mirrored in his right hand. He tried again and again, even reverting to blunt force – but to no avail, the knife simply wouldn't fit. Finally he switched hands; the moment he held the knife in his right hand it slid easily into the sheath, now held in his left.

This experience taught him that from now on, he's better off holding a knife in his right hand. Thus continues the conditioning process – until a child may no longer know if they are left- or right-handed. They stand to lose touch with their natural disposition, which can lead to a sense of disorder or even confusion.

I am amazed how often righties ask me what the big deal is – if a lefty can learn to do things with their right hand, where's the problem? My answer is simple: Try to do everything with your left hand for a week, and you'll see what it's like!

Here's another example: I once got talking with a left-handed dentist who had fought his way through his own valley of despair. During his training he only had instruments for right-handed use, as none existed for lefties! Not surprisingly, he made slower progress than his colleagues and failed several exams. In the end he managed to master use of these specialized instruments with his right hand, and has since established his own successful practice. But can you imagine what it must be like to carry out high-precision work with your "passive" hand?

One of my students was great at "jamming" with me on the Djembe (an African drum you play with your hands). He appeared to be keeping a casual eye on me; but I know this kind of look and intuitively guessed how intensively he was watching my every move. We played the same rhythm for some time – and as soon as I stopped, he abruptly stopped as well. When I asked him to keep going in the same rhythm he was unable to do so – he had been closely mirroring my playing, but couldn't remember or re-create a single pattern himself.

We repeated this a few times until we broke down in laughter at the comical situation – jamming together was great, but the second I stopped, so did he. Once we stopped laughing, though, my student confessed that he forgot a lot of regular things in his daily life – even simple stuff! He had developed a routine to compensate for this before anybody could notice, honing his observation skills to the point where he could effortlessly follow along and blend in.

You could argue that his ability for perfect, instant imitation is a special skill. But for me, this imitation means he's lacking a vital connection to what he's actually doing. Or in the case of the Djembe, he's not consciously playing himself, but only following someone else's lead – and doesn't actually know what he's doing.

Let me pause here to make a confession: This reminds me what it was like in the first few bands I played with. When I was 18, I played in a cover band (mostly dance music). I could never remember songs and how they went, but could react amazingly quickly to changes – stops, breaks, etc. This earned me the reputation of being a "very musical" drummer who could play almost anything. But in reality this "talent" was my acute sense of listening for and quickly reacting to cues, which I had honed as a mechanism to compensate for my lack of ability to remember or even understand what I was playing. I would never have been able to take the lead in any song! The moment someone else kicked off a new song I was right there with them, but I could never have been the backbone for any band.

We've talked about natural disposition, and I hope you're still on board with me. In case I've left you wondering what the point is – what this natural disposition to use your left vs. your right hand means – let me answer that by digging a little more into the characteristics of "right" and "left". The two stand in natural tension to each other, which creates a kind of polarity in our own bodies. I'll explain more about this in the next chapter.

2. POLARITY

Polarity is all around us: Hot and cold, high and low pressure, plus and minus, light and dark. Asian philosophy describes this as "Ying" and "Yang", which belong together and create one unity. One cannot exist without the other. Take a battery, for example, with its positive and negative poles. It needs the essential tension these two poles create – if one was missing, there's no way the battery could do its thing.

Important: The "positive" isn't more important than the "negative", there isn't a "good" or "bad" side; let's relegate that to comic books where good fights evil, or Westerns where the cowboys in the white hats always defeat their counterparts in black. For the rest of our discussion, let's move forward free of judgement.

You can find polarity in several places in the human body – we'll focus on the right and left sides. The natural tension between these two sides creates energy – which a drummer taps into to create "groove".

Try it out yourself: If you play a series of beats with one hand, or even tap a simple rhythm with only one hand, the polarity is missing. No groove can develop. The beats – in this case a string of single impulses – could just as well have been produced by a drum machine.

Now, play the same series of beats or tap that same simple rhythm with both hands. The moment you switch to using both hands you automatically create that tension – and your playing opens up. Did you feel the difference?

Your audience certainly does. In the first example, the audience perceives a certain drive, a forward motion. But the moment both hands come into play, it's like the lid is blown off – we tap into an additional force, the rhythm gains a new dimension and starts to groove.

And… once you develop a sense for how your body moves through space you can even add a third dimension to your playing. This further intensifies the impact you can have on those around you – the audience and your fellow band-members. Space and time are linked; the more awareness you develop for your movements through space, the more precision you can bring to your drumming. Honing your awareness of your movements through space can help you achieve the natural point in time which not only is, but more importantly _feels_ correct.

I'll come back down to earth now and make this a bit easier to grasp: Let's do another experiment.

Try to play steady even beats at a slow pace.
It's easier if you use expansive, exaggerated movements. It's kind of like jumping on a trampoline: You'll naturally discover just the right height to fit with any tempo. The higher you jump, the slower; conversely, the faster you jump, the lower.

Resist your temptation to control your movements – allow your sticks to fall into a natural rhythm without any controlled force from your side. The rebound you feel from the drumhead comes together with the speed and height of your arm movements to become one, enabling you to hold a steady beat. Once you have mastered this, you will have found the balance between the space and timing of your beats.

You may have noticed that a lot of modern drummers play with large, expansive arm movements. They don't just do it for show – but to increase the energy in their playing. Space contains a lot of energy for us to tap into when we play. This intensifies your stage-presence, making your audience more aware of you. It's not about playing louder – that's a secondary effect.

Some drummers play quietly in spite of their huge movements, which at first glance don't seem to line up at all! They "brake" their motion at the last second, as if they wanted to gently place their sticks on the drumhead. Some even play with "quieter" drumsticks made of lighter wood with thinner heads. Others even reach to rods or brushes to balance out their expansive movements so as to not sacrifice intense energy when playing quietly.

The polarity I spoke of at the beginning of this chapter can also be found in our on-board computers: Our brains. Each of our brain's hemispheres has different tasks and functions – but let's take a short break, I'll go into a bit more detail on that in the next chapter.

3. OUR TWO BRAIN HEMISPHERES

The human brain is essentially divided into two hemispheres, or halves. (Actually, our brains are way more complex than that! For the purposes of our discussion, let's keep it simple and focus on the high-level categorization right-brain and left-brain).

Basically, we can picture each hemisphere as having one principle characteristic attributed to it: I'll refer to them as "rational" (also called conscious, or logical thought) and "sub-conscious" (also called emotional, or intuition).

In a right-handed person's brain the left hemisphere is the "rational" center, and the right hemisphere the "emotional". For lefties, though, it's the other way around – our right-brains are the center of our rational thought. You may have also heard the terms cerebrum (rational) and cerebellum (subconscious) – they're another way of referring to these two hemispheres.

Medical science defines left-handedness as the reversed functionality or allocation of our two brain halves. Recent research studies are investigating possible causes for left-handedness such as genetics or hereditary factors. However, research into left-handedness is still in its infancy. The major hurdle is the lack of experience for researchers to tap into – two generations ago there simply weren't any lefties! It wasn't "accepted" to be left-handed, as using your left hand was considered unclean, wrong, or even the devil's work! I've done a lot of looking around in my circle of friends and acquaintances. It seems that each family I know who has a left-handed child has at least one person in the prior generation who was also a lefty. My own family seems to follow this rule, too: Unfortunately I don't have children of my own, but one of my two nephews is a lefty and my father – although he denies being left-handed – plays soccer with his left foot; in addition, (sorry, Dad!) he completely lacks fine motor skills when using his right hand.

This basic division of the brain into two hemispheres can help make certain characteristics and occurrences more tangible:

- For righties, the "rational" left-brain is linked to the right hand, which is also the active or dominant hand
- Their left hand is therefore linked to the right-brain, or the "subconscious" side
- Logically, this is flipped for lefties

For drumming, this means:

- Right-handed drummers use their right hand as their leading hand, and the left hand follows
- Left-handed drummers experience the opposite: Their left hand is their leading hand, and the right hand follows

We have immediate, direct control over our leading hand, while our following hand often feels somewhat detached or passive. I've often heard students say "I don't really have any feeling in that hand!" This isn't entirely correct, as often our best path to our leading hand is via <u>feeling</u>. This term is often misunderstood!

Let me try to explain what feeling means to me: We are so used to feeling complete control over our leading hand that our logical self expects this same level of control – this same <u>feeling</u> in our following hand, too. In this context, "feeling" refers to the perception of being in control, rather than the other meaning of feeling: "Sensing" something in an intuitive way. If you let go and allow your following hand to "feel" rather than "control", though, you can discover a strong, unique role for your following hand. For drummers, this means finding the naturally opposing pole to your lead hand. And if you remember our talk about polarity – you understand how much energy this can unlock for your playing!

Unfortunately, this poses one of the greatest obstacles in the path to virtuous drumming. We drummers can only truly develop when we discover and embrace our following hand's natural role – which is <u>not</u> a mere copy of our leading hand! As long as we try to train our passive and active hands to play exactly the same way, we are destined to frustration.

To be successful, allow yourself to tap into all your senses; both your rational and your subconscious need to be free to do their thing. In order to really use your brain – all of it – sometimes you need to stop thinking so hard.

4. IT ALL BEGINS WITH THE "1"

The "1" is what we call the first beat of a measure. It's a typical downbeat; rhythmically speaking it's the beginning and also the end of any piece of music. Have you ever tried to end a song on the "4"? And wondered why you didn't get any applause? Your audience was missing closure – because the "4" feels like it's leading back to the "1". Especially in European-based cultures, the "1" is the most important beat of the measure. The bass drum places a clear accent on the "1" when we play a march or a waltz. We clap on the "1", and when we dance, we move on the "1". This first beat represents a kind of grounding; through its strength and weight it gives us the feeling that everything is in order.

Naturally we play the "1" with our leading hand: A right-handed drummer wouldn't achieve the optimal energy level for a "1" if they had to strike with their left hand. The "1" should feel powerful, heavy and grounded – and come just a touch too late, like the bass drum in a marching band. An accent on the "1" played with the wrong hand on a drum set (for example on the crash cymbal) is missing natural energy and won't achieve the desired effect; it feels "thin", random and unimportant. Only our leading hand can unleash the full potential of this powerful beat.

A clear "1" is essential for controlled playing; if we play the "1" with our weaker hand we risk a sense of disorientation creeping into our play. This can lead to real difficulties reading music, challenges recognizing the beginning and ending of a measure, the inability to place fills correctly … this lack of orientation snowballs until we lose our sense of timing and can't keep an even tempo.
But above all – we end up stifling our natural "groove".

5. GROOVE AND TENSION

Groove is energy! It's that intangible feeling our audience and other band members get when we play, it's what pulls them in and keeps them hooked. I talked about this in the Polarity chapter: The natural tension between our right and left hand, between the right and left sides of our body is at the heart of groove. It's unleashed by the energy field created between our two hands – energy that can't develop if we play all beats with just one hand.

Playing with both hands creates a kind of natural conflict: The downbeats and upbeats have opposite energy which gives each its own character. Typical marching music is a great example: The first beat is undeniably a "down-beat" – who doesn't feel a natural downward motion in their body? The next beat is an "upbeat" – carrying our bodies back upwards again.

Try this: Play a very simple march beat in 2/4 time the "wrong way around": Give the downbeat with your weak hand instead of your leading hand. Can't you feel the lack of energy, how it doesn't feel quite right? You can also try playing the same simple march beat with just one hand; here too you'll feel how the natural tension is missing.

We can create this tension at the drum set – which helps us achieve "groove" – by introducing different kinds of "natural conflicts":

- Left foot on the bass drum and right hand on the snare drum (or the other way around for right-handed drummers)
- Tuning the bass drum deeper and the snare drum higher
- Coming in late on the bass drum and early on the snare drum (or the other way around, depending on tempo and style)

Some drummers like to further intensify these "natural conflicts" by tuning their drum set to the extreme, for example tuning the snare drum very high. Another approach is to strike the snare drum as early as possible. Have you ever noticed that in certain songs you tend to come in slightly late on the snare? It takes a lot of practice to hit the snare early without coming in early on the bass drum, too... which would kill the very polarity we're working to achieve.

Coming in slightly late on the bass drum is the key to expressive playing when it comes to binary playing in songs with a medium tempo. A strong, rich bass drum doesn't come from playing loudly, but through the effect created by exact placement of your beats. This control requires giving the role of the bass drum to your leading foot – for us lefties, that's our left foot!

Here's something else for you to try: Pick a passage where you play the bass drum exaggeratedly late and record yourself playing. Then, compare the feeling you got while playing with the feeling you had while listening. I'll bet you struggled while you were playing and thought there's no way it could sound right! But I'll also bet that when you went back and listened, you were surprised by how even and "normal" it sounded, ignoring of course your own uncertainty as you played.

6. GROOVE AND THE JOY OF DRUMMING

The energy your audience feels when you play isn't generated solely from this tension, but also from the joy you experience while playing. I'm sure you've witnessed drummers who produce a great effect through their very presence and appearance; you could almost remove the sound track and still be left with a fantastic impression!

The positive emotions you feel while playing are sparks which leap over to ignite your audience, and can only be set free if you have a positive energy flow. How can you tap into this positive energy? Ensure proper posture and remove any obstacles which stand in the way of your natural flow. This means paying particular attention to:

- Your sitting position (how you hold your back, head, shoulders and chest)
- How you hold your arms
- Your shoulder, elbow and wrist movements
- The height of your seat (the proper angles of your legs, knees, ankles and feet)

Tell me this: How could it possibly be worth the investment to work with an instructor and fine-tune all these details, only to play on drums set up opposite to your true nature? That would strangle any positive energy flow before it has a chance to develop; the true joy of playing would get lost along the way.

At this point you may argue that there are many drummers out there who play Open Hand or even "the wrong way around", yet still play with energy and joy. My answer? How much more intense would their energy and their enjoyment be if they were to play the "right way around" -?!

Allow me to share my own personal experience: I played Open Hand for 20 years, during which I enjoyed drumming and thought I felt the "groove". However, what I felt then was nothing in comparison to what I experienced <u>after</u> switching sides!

In the course of those 20 years I used to look forward to practicing. However, the longer I sat at my drum set practicing, the less enthusiastic I felt; my practice sessions often left me feeling empty and sluggish. My vitality didn't grow as I played, but kind of fizzled out. Since I re-built my drum set the other way around everything flipped around for me – now I can sit down at my drums feeling annoyed, stressed and even "empty"; yet as I practice my enjoyment increases. I feel relaxed yet full of drive – at peace with the world.

This sense of vitality is even more important when you are playing on stage. Not only does it win over your audience and drive the band, it's also crucial for your own playing. Only when you feel this intense enjoyment while playing can you surrender yourself to the music, letting it course through you rather than intellectually trying to control it. Anyone who has played on stage can empathize with how hard it can be, yet how critical it is to "let go". Trust me – this is a big deal!

7. TYPICAL SHORTCOMINGS

Unfortunately, the following shortcomings are typical for left-handed drummers who play on right-handed drum sets:

- Serious difficulties reading music
- A sense of aimlessness within songs and arrangements
- Weak sense for the length, beginning and end of fills
- Fills which lack intention, feel "haphazard"
- Rehearsed sequences are quickly forgotten (they are saved in the wrong brain hemisphere)
- Accents played with the crash cymbal aren't placed convincingly, lack energy
- Practicing and mastering skills and songs takes significantly longer (which may go unnoticed due to lack of comparison)
- Quick to tire, which leads to lack of drive and even exhaustion
- Lack of dependability when playing together with other musicians, which is also felt as a sense of uncertainty

- Pre-occupied with themselves because their own playing robs the bulk of their attention – leaving little room for perceiving the other musicians or the audience
- The drummer's leadership role suffers immensely, to the point of being non-existent

I've often observed that lefties tend to experience a general lack of orientation in every-day life, giving the impression we're a bit "scatter-brained". This comes from our limbs not having clearly assigned roles. Missing this natural order can leave us with a sense of confusion; we lose our ability to recognize the simple things, and end up over-thinking things which we make more complicated than they need to be.

8. PENCHANT FOR OVERTHINKING

It's striking how some of my left-handed drum students trained the "wrong way around" developed an "over-analytical" style of playing. Each stroke felt controlled and "artificial", as if they were playing with the handbrake on – lacking power, energy and expression.

Several have opened up to me in personal conversations, and I find it remarkable how many of them experience this same phenomenon in every-day life. They often describe it along these lines: They take such a rational approach to every decision they make that it ends up as an exhausting chore. They drag every possible (and even some impossible) alternatives into consideration, playing out countless scenarios and weighing endless risks against potential outcomes. And here comes the ironic part – in hindsight, they feel that more often than not they ended up making the wrong decision! Yet simply making a decision based on "gut-feel" wasn't an option.

Why is that?

Because many of us lefties aren't familiar with what a "gut feel" feels like. Years of using the "opposite" brain hemispheres prevents us from feeling "grounded", which blocks the reassuring feeling that everything is cruising along just fine. In a brain with correct polarity, things that naturally fall into the subconscious (where intuition rules) end up in the rationally thinking hemisphere, leading us to pore over things which should be decided instinctively.

Life gets a lot easier when we let ourselves make simple decisions intuitively! Trust me, you can rely on your subconscious to make decisions more often than you think. Over time, we can learn which important tasks are best delegated to our precious "rationale" and which are best left to take care of themselves through intuition.

What this means for drummers:

Drumming doesn't come from the "head"! It's not our reason, but our intuition that guides our playing as we tap into movements we've committed to muscle memory through dedicated practice. This allows us stay relaxed – both in mind and body. As I've said earlier, this ability to relax and "let go" is key to achieving flow and energy in your playing.

This frees up your "head" for other important things:
- Listening to your own playing, so you can make adjustments or align with others
- Listening to other musicians, keeping eye contact, being open for their gestures and expressions
- Paying attention to your audience; noticing their reactions and the signals they give
- Reading your music

- Focusing on the song's sequences, knowing what comes next

9. TYPES OF LEFTIES

Now that we've looked at the hurdles lefties face while growing up, it's easier to explain how different types of lefties emerge. Please take the following types as examples, based on my experience observing and teaching lefties. They also exist among right-handed people (and in hidden lefties living as righties, too)! The following types described here aren't exhaustive, I'm sure there are other types, sub-types and combinations out there too.

Please note: I'm not a scientist, and this isn't based on scientific study. But I'm not making things up, either – this chapter is based on human traits I've encountered through interacting with and observing scores of students. Hopefully I can help you better understand people who show these traits, so you can connect with and instruct them more effectively. Besides – who knows – maybe the odd reader will even recognize themselves in the following passages.

The Fighter

This type has had to make things happen in their life – and has been successful. They perceive their life as a fight: "Me vs. the rest of the world". Their drumming achievements didn't come easily, but required a lot of work. Consistently challenged with new hurdles, they've only been able to overcome them with a huge investment in practice time and effort. Their patience, perseverance and hard work are remarkable; not to mention their inner drive! This type generally reach the goals they strive toward – albeit very slowly and with disproportionate effort on their part. These successes are achieved so slowly that they often go unnoticed; only after a long period of time can any notable progress be seen.

The Fighter wants to prove something to themselves and to the world: They can do it! They can be good, maybe even the best; at the very least, they can be something special.

These people are often taxing to be around. Sure they can be interesting and likable, and their penchant to look for a deeper meaning behind common things gives them a certain depth of character. Yet their constant questioning, their drive to "prove themselves" gets annoying over time! At some point their ambition and drive to lead the crowd becomes too much, creating negative pressure instead of enthusiasm.

When faced with a challenge they tend to attack full-on, which is often as effective as banging their head against a brick wall. They don't have an intrinsic sense of "lightness of being", don't know how to relax and let themselves "surf" the natural flow. It's a real shame they don't realize that reducing, not increasing pressure can be the key to success – relaxing until you resonate with natural harmony is a more effective way to succeed.

I've personally experienced the profound impact that re-learning to play drums the "other way around" – giving the lead to your naturally strong hand – has made on the lives of these Fighters. One of my students told me how his outlook on life completely changed once he had crossed the "valley of despair" and begun to make real progress. (I've dedicated a chapter to this valley a bit later on). Many aspects of his life aside from drumming had become tangibly lighter. Amazingly he started getting much better results at University than ever before – with less effort! His friends noticed the change too, and described him as much easier to be around. Hc'd matured into a relaxed, cool guy.

The Dreamer

This group has created their own parallel universe, born of the desire to escape a world which they perceive as hard, heartless and full of barriers. They refuse to do battle with the rest of the world, choosing instead to cocoon themselves in a romanticized, cozy dream world. They see obstacles everywhere they look; they can't discern any given plan or order in their environment.

They avoid conflict and seem elusive to their peers – the more you try to nail them down, the better they elude you and slip away. We're left shaking our heads, wondering how they make it through life without a grasp of the obvious – how often do they stand directly in front of something without seeing it? When we explain something they usually miss the point and just don't get it. Others tend to avoid them, it's tiring to be with someone you simply can't get through to! Their presence isn't disruptive, but uncomfortable – they take our attention and energy but don't give anything in return. You could say they soak up their environment – I call people like this "sponges".

The experiences that come with re-learning to play the drums with the dominant hand can help Dreamers connect with the world in a more meaningful way. A natural playing style helps to personally experience the natural laws governing the universe: We sense natural forces such as rebound, tension in the sticks, space and time and feel what it's like when our bodies interact with them. The dream world slowly gives way to a visceral contact with the real world, the boundaries between internal and external slowly dissolve. This new relationship between internal and external impulses enables a re-awakening, the former "Dreamer" becomes more firmly anchored in the real world. And to their delight, life takes on a fresh new glow as positive experiences replace negative ones. Exchanging their negative world view with a neutral, unbiased one helps them realize their full creative potential.

This re-awakening has an amazing impact on how they play the drums. Their former feeling of playing through a filter is replaced with freshness, they truly connect with their audience and fellow band members. Music is no longer an escape from the real world – they are finally open to truly hear and enjoy their own playing.

The Chaotic Meanderer

This group wanders aimlessly through daily life without any concrete goal or plan, mixing things up along the way. They don't focus on any one specific thing and avoid fully exploring or understanding things. Instead, they steer clear of this kind of study – it could be they discover something uncomfortable about themselves which calls for change… but change requires too much work, and is be avoided at all costs! Quick to try new things, they never explore them in depth, and are even notorious for abandoning new hobbies.

Chaotic Meanderers are friendly and fun to be with and don't take themselves too seriously. They want to be well-liked, so don't burden others with their struggle to set or meet goals. Ironically, this leaves them oblivious to their messes, leaving a trail of missed appointments and mixed up dates in their wake! They simply turn a blind eye, ignoring or even rejecting natural order not only in their own lives, but in the world around them.

As you can imagine, their drumming doesn't have any clear structure – no leading hand, no following hand. There's no way for natural order to take root in their playing. Yet establishing structure in their playing can open the door to discovering their true characteristics and personality, leading to substantial change in their every-day lives. What a wonderful gift to finally discover our roots in such a way that we can confidently establish our own point of view, no longer concerned about what others will think.

Their former penchant for dabbling in many things gives way to focused dedication as they discover how fulfilling it can be to devote yourself to one real passion. This paves the way to developing an impressive identity among their peers as well as a strong drumming personality: Aimlessness is replaced by expressiveness, character and power.

10. READING MUSIC

Most of the left-handed drummers I know really have a hard time reading music. It only gets worse when they play with a right-handed setup – in that situation, playing to written marks on paper can spiral into a seemingly impossible task! But even those who play with their drum set the "right way around" often struggle with this. In fact, I've seen reading deficits among many of my students who tell me how they struggle with reading, grammar and literature at school. For me, the root of the problem lies in a lack of structure, as well as failure to recognize how things are organized. In music, this carries over to beats – left-handed students often lack the ability to see organization or a sense of order across a set of measures.

I've developed a method for helping my lefty students overcome this difficulty reading music, using this approach:

(1) Every note stands in relationship to the "1" (the first beat in a measure).
(2) If you can't feel the "1", you can't feel where any of the other notes should be.
(3) Every note in a measure has its own rhythmic character, which needs to be learned.
(4) Reading music isn't a rote exercise in reading symbols on paper, but rather a process of converting recognized symbols

into physical experiences we have committed to (muscle) memory when we play.

See what I mean?
Here's some examples:

You see an apple: But you don't think of the letters a-p-p-l-e. Instead, you think of its taste, which you know from having eaten many apples.

You see a street sign: You know a yellow triangle with children doesn't mean there are children standing on the road – but you instinctively step on the brake to avoid getting a speeding ticket in a school zone! Not only was that drilled into you during driving school; experience has also firmly anchored its meaning in your memory.

It's the same with reading music. The notes serve as symbols, there to help trigger a specific response: A particular rhythm or figure you have already learned how to play. After re-building their drum set to lead with left, left-handed drummers quickly gains a sense of organization and order in their playing; as a result reading music becomes easier.

Sound hard to believe? Let me tell you about my own experience:

A few months after I re-built my drum set "the other way around", my teacher came in one day and placed a sheet of music on my stand. Not just any sheet of music, but my nemesis – a song which I had honestly grown to hate after lots of struggling and many failed attempts to play it correctly.

"Let's give this a shot", he said.

"Really?" I thought. I have to admit this song had consistently kicked my butt… not only had I been unable to play a single line correctly, but I kept making mistakes – it just took a few measures for me to completely lose my orientation and bail out.

By this point we'd been working on my re-orientation for months, and it had been at least half a year since I had read any music at all (something I hadn't missed in the least!) As you can imagine, being confronted not only with sheet music – but this hated song – really sank my spirits. "Come on," I protested, "you know I can't play this!"

"Let's just give it a shot", he repeated.

We played the opening measures together, then the rest of the first line, then the second line, third line… until we had played the whole piece. Without one single mistake.

We both sat for a moment in silence, staring at the music. Then my teacher turned to me. "Thomas… ?"

"I have no idea what just happened", I admitted. "I haven't looked at a sheet of music for months, let alone practiced sight-reading. You know that's not something I'm fond of." We were both astonished at what had just happened.

Since then I've had similar experiences with many of my students. Each time it's an unforgettable moment, for them as well as for me. The first couple of times it seemed like an incredible phenomenon – something beyond any explanation. Now, though, I see it differently; it's perfectly logical. You see: The students had seen lots of notes, and had understood the principle of what they meant. The mental work had been done, they had learned that lesson. The problem lay in the implementation. How could a drummer put this learning into practice while struggling against their natural tendencies? In that case reading music remains a "cerebral" exercise, when you over-think at some point you just shut down; often after just a line or two.

When I speak of "cerebral", I'm referring to the rational hemisphere of our brains. Each stroke must be "thought through", the concentration required is really hard work for our rationale! Did you know that the Latin word "concentra" means focusing on your own center? That's not our heads, but the center of our bodies – our "gut" (which can be compared with "Hara" and "Tanden" in Japanese culture). In recent years Western Medicine has discovered and attributed more importance to this form of intelligence in the center of our bodies; we allocate thinking to our subconscious and follow our "gut feeling".

11. RIGHT OR LEFT-HANDED?

Drum instructors are often faced with the question whether a student is right or left-handed. Honestly, determining this shouldn't be the responsibility of a teacher. In case of doubt the student should instead seek advice from a specialist; for example from psychologists specialized in this area who can conduct qualifying tests.

As I mentioned earlier, many people are "switched" during childhood, when they are conditioned from an early age to conform to a right-handed world. Some lefties have simply resigned and accepted that everything works "right" – they don't make any effort to re-position things to better suit them. I've often witnessed lefties sitting down at a right-handed drum set without second-guessing it.

A lot of emphasis is placed on the role of the left and right hands during lessons. This can bring the issue of left-handedness to the forefront – putting the onus on the instructor to determine if a student may indeed be a lefty. In this situation, they carry an enormous responsibility. In my mind, teaching a student who you know to be left-handed to play on a right-handed drum set is nothing less than PHYSICAL ASSULT!

How can an instructor determine if a student is left-handed?

1) Ask your student

If your student already knows they are left-handed, there is absolutely no reason to teach them to play right-handed. ABSOLUTELY. NO. REASON.
In case you wonder why I'm so insistent on this point, let me share a list of weak excuses I've encountered over the years, together with my counter-arguments:

- It's too much of a hassle to re-build the drum set every time.
  What kind of teacher would say this? Isn't our instruction for the sake of our students -??

- Drum sets are always set up that way on stage; you can't expect them to be re-configured every time, that would lead to a disadvantage for the left-handed player. *Trust me, re-configuring takes exactly 2 minutes, and I often use this time to my advantage.*

- You can't reconfigure a drum set.
  Please. The drum set is probably the only instrument you <u>can</u> re-configure, and easily!

- That would mean the drummer looks in the wrong direction.
  "Wrong" direction? It's just the "other" direction. The bands I've played with get used to this very quickly. In fact, one jazz musician first complained it was strange having me on the "other side" – but told me later it felt just as strange when he went back to playing with a right-handed drummer. We may be creatures of habit, but we adapt quickly!

- The position of the other band members would need to be changed accordingly.
  This one does have a root of truth – band members need to look the other way to make eye contact. Thank goodness our necks let us swivel our heads in both directions! Besides, my experience has shown that standing in different positions on stage can open new perspectives for the band.

2) Hearing test, volume

Stand with your back to your student and have them play a series of strokes on a practice pad. You'll soon hear a stronger and a weaker stroke –

which clearly identifies the leading and following hands.

3) Hearing test, timing

Here, the teacher identifies one hand's stroke as "direct", while in comparison the other is slightly "stuck". The direct stroke comes slightly earlier, while the "stuck" stroke limps behind, dragging just a bit. The leading hand is always more direct and feels "fresher" – as it comes from the controlling side. The following hand carries a more indirect signature, feels somehow more passive.

4) Observation of arm movement while walking

Have your student walk a few steps, "as casually as possible". Watch their arms very carefully – do both arms swing freely and in synch with the gait? It's actually quite rare for someone to swing both arms equally freely – usually one side "sticks" slightly.

Try this: Next time you're out in a crowd, watch people as they walk by. Most of the time you'll see one arm swinging freely while the other hangs still; maybe the person is carrying a bag, or has their hand in their pocket. In most cases the side which swings freely is the "leading" side – so for righties, their right arm. The subconscious side of the body, where dormant fears, problems or stress are carried, is "stuck".

For many of us, it feels odd to let our "other" side swing freely. Doing so would be healthy, as it would help us free ourselves of a lot of baggage! Letting both arms swing freely feels very odd at first: We feel like a bit of a clown as the former stiffness gives way to what seems like exaggerated swinging. But stick with it – and in time you'll feel grounded in yourself, as the external "control" (generated by activating your arm muscles) gives way to a feeling of inner stability.

5) Observation of playing style, shoulders

In some cases both shoulders aren't equally relaxed when drumming, so they aren't level with each other. A slightly crooked posture can give valuable hints as to which side is dominant – in this case, the "active" side is usually pulled somewhat higher while the "passive" side hangs a bit lower.

6) Observation of playing style, wrists

Once again, ask your student to play a series of strokes on the practice pad. The student's passive wrist is often pulled closer in to the core of their body, the arm gets "stuck". On the other, active side the feeling of having to "take charge" can result in using too much power and the arm shows more movement; on the active side the wrist tends to be held straighter.

7) Grooving: Hearing test

Have your student only play bass and snare drum. Begin with the right foot on the bass drum and the left hand on the snare. Then have them play the other way around. You will probably be able to perceive which version "grooves" better – the version which yields more energy on the downbeat (bass drum) and a fresher, lighter upbeat on the snare drum.

8) Grooving: Feeling

Ask your student how they perceive playing bass drum with each of their feet: They should be able to feel which foot leads to a stronger sense of the beat being anchored in their core. A beat played with the wrong foot feels artificial, whereas you can feel how a beat played with the leading foot is driven by power that originates in your "guts".

This is best done by asking your student to play a typical march in 2/4 time – downbeat and upbeat. How does each version feel – downbeat with the left or right foot, upbeat with the right or left hand? Which version releases the most energy into the march? Which way would they play intuitively?

9) Have at it!

For this test, start off with practice pads – have your student start drumming! Quickly call out a series of different strokes for them to play. Which hand do they begin with instinctively? You can even move this exercise onto a drum set if you like and watch what happens. Does your student, while sitting at a right-handed drum set, ever begin with their left hand? If so, that's a pretty big sign they may be left-handed – when playing alternating strokes the move from one drum to the next (the one situated to the right) comes naturally and easily when you begin with the right hand. But if you begin with the left hand, the switch is more difficult.

Here's an old parlor trick: Ask someone to cross their arms. Allegedly a righty will place their left arm in front and their right arm against their body; the lefty will do just the opposite – place their left arm against their body and the right arm in front. In my experience, though, this often leads to false results.

That said, I still like asking people to cross their arms, then I ask if they're right or left-handed. This has helped me discover a lot of stories: Those who were switched, who do things with both hands, or who haven't ever thought of it before. It's amazing how rarely this topic is addressed – even though it's so important for each and every one of us.

12. THE LIGHTNESS OF BEING

When the critical factors fall into place – when we lead with our natural hand and achieve polarity in our playing – we unleash a special energy which those around us perceive as "groove" or "power". Sometimes we musicians don't perceive this energy as strongly as our listeners. I've often experienced lessons where the room was flooded with an amazing energy; paradoxically, the very source of this energy – the drummer – didn't even notice!

This energy which we release – I'll call this outward-focused energy, is often accompanied by an opposite force: Energy directed within, which I'll call inward-focused energy. I've long wondered if drummers are able to perceive outward-focused energy at all, and have come to the conclusion that we only perceive the inward-focused force.

In any case, we as musicians should develop a sensitivity towards both energy forms, which can serve not only as an indicator if all is going well and we're "grooving – but also as a way to delve deeper into the music. That's when we have even more fun, and our body movements naturally become more harmonious and aligned with what we're doing. We may even experience a kind of rush which releases a feeling of utter happiness (all 100% drug-free!) Not only is this state incredibly pleasurable, it's also healthy!

These moments allow us to experience a feeling of unity: With our music, our fellow band members, the audience, the room… everything around us. Everything seems so simple, so clear, so easy. It all just feels right, "clicks" – and we're part of it. I know this may sound pretty esoteric to many of you – but I'll bet those who've experienced this feeling would agree with me. Once you've felt this state, if only for a moment, you automatically crave more: You'd love to feel this more often; if you could, all the time!

This sets a process in motion: Our personal perception of the world around us makes a great leap forward. We notice that our priorities shift; our search for gratification in the form of acquiring more possessions or striving towards positions of power suddenly lose their charm. We feel emotionally more balanced and satisfied. We seek more opportunities where we can experience this "lightness of being"; we can't get enough! Every day, every interaction becomes a new opportunity to dive into this newly discovered state.

Our every-day lives settle into a comfortable routine, our stress dissipates and our fight against time evolves into a sense of flowing with time. Pleasant surprises and coincidences come our way more often, opportunities arise and we notice that the right things come along at the right time. We see things from a different perspective, yet remain firmly anchored in the here and now. Our musical instrument has become another kind of instrument: An aide in our own personal development as we adopt a new role in the world, or even partake in a new world – one often described in books, essays and poems. A world which many don't believe exists. For me, it does.

13. PLAYING WITH A METRONOME

I have often noticed that lefties have unique issues when it comes to playing with a metronome. The problem lies in an innately weak feeling for the "1" (which I described in an earlier chapter) and thus a poorly developed sense of grounding in this critically important beat. Left-handed drummers often don't know what it feels like to let yourself fall into the "1"; we work so hard to "make" this first beat, forcing it to come in synch with the metronome. This usually turns into a difficult, frustrating journey. But before I make any suggestions, I'd like to make a few background observations about playing with a metronome:

Basics on playing with a metronome

On the one hand, it's critically important for a drummer to be able to play accurately with a metronome. But on the other hand, practicing with a metronome can be counter-productive or even destructive. Drummers use metronomes to help establish an internal sense of timing so steadfast that it becomes a reliable gut feel; only then can bands rely on them.

That said, practicing with a metronome carries the risk of interfering with or even preventing that goal. Instead of the drummer developing their inner sense of timing, they can instead become a slave to timing dictated by an external source.

When a drummer can't play an even, steady beat without a metronome, that's a pretty good sign they're on the wrong path. The right path would be using the metronome as an aid to help develop an internal sense of timing. How do we do this?

First of all, think of the metronome as an external support. When practicing, don't concentrate too hard on hitting every beat exactly on the click. Instead, focus on your own inner timing, and try to compare that with the clicks you hear. Try playing a while without the metronome. Once you feel that you're really "in" the groove, your inner timing is probably pretty firmly established. Now's the right time to turn on the metronome. Then, keep playing with that same "in the groove" sense of timing. It can be really helpful to record your playing at this point.

Did you feel your timing was on, but the metronome revealed you were playing too quickly? That means your own perception isn't aligned with the "correct" timing. Try to work on your own sense of timing while you play; in this case, try "breaking" to slow yourself down. Once you've found the groove again, it's time to compare with the metronome a second time. How are you doing? Still too fast? Or have you gotten too slow? Or are you "in time"? Keep repeating this process until your inner sense of timing matches what the metronome tells you. Focus on what that feels like – this "correct" timing. This process will gradually strengthen your feeling for timing.

Once you feel secure in your timing, move on to the next step. For example, try out what it feels like when you speed up on purpose, or when you "lay back" and slow down the beat. In either case, continue checking in periodically with the metronome.

Exercises for lefties

To help you establish a secure inner sense of timing, start off with just the pedal and the metronome – this will help you establish a sense of timing with your left foot. As you do this, let yourself feel the time intervals, the space between the clicks. You can do this simply by tapping your foot on the floor, or start with the bass drum.

The next step is to repeat this exercise with your left hand, using a stick and a practice pad. Playing directly on the snare will be too loud, you won't be able to hear the precise moment of your strike and won't be able to judge if it's in time with the click.

Once you've got that down, move on to the next step: Place strikes in between with your right hand. Keep your left foot on the bass drum (or your left hand on the practice pad) in time with the metronome clicks, and place your right hand in between. How does the timing feel now? And the space between clicks? Try to focus your full attention on the movement of your stick through space. When you move your stick as slowly and precisely as possible, do you feel the spaces between clicks more strongly?

This feeling for the space between clicks is fundamentally important. I'd even go so far as to say it's THE one true reference point. After all, drumming is principally made up of large movements through space and specific points in time. Investing time to hone your perception of these two factors won't only enhance your drumming, but your overall interaction with time and space.

When practicing with the metronome, I recommend reducing your tempo step by step; your feeling for space in time between clicks is much stronger in when you play very slowly. Try playing for example 60 BPM (beats per minute) with your left foot: Make sure you always let yourself "fall into" each click, allow an exaggerated sense of sluggishness in your body. Pay attention to not force your strikes, but instead try to minimize your own action and stay as passive as possible; be patient and wait for what seems like an eternity between beats. This will help you learn to rely on your inner clock.

14. IN HARMONY

In this chapter, I'd like to go into more detail about a phenomenon which many seasoned drummers have shared with me. Their descriptions usually go something like this: While practicing or during a performance they suddenly felt an amazing power channel through their body; it was as if they totally "took off", experiencing an incredible rush.

It's hard to describe this sensation in words – other than to say that it's not unlike being high. Your timing is perfect, the band has melded together, the audience is going wild. It's like you're under a spell. Once you've felt this, you naturally yearn for more. You'll probably wonder "what was that"? And ask yourself "how do I get it again? What happened to me, what can I do, drink or take?"

Some think taking drugs can lead them back to this state. Nope – that's a dead-end road.

It's not a chemical intoxication, but rather a special kind of consciousness or enhanced perception. You are entirely "one" with yourself and with the world around you. Instructors who have personally experienced this can serve as a guide by helping you set the right parameters to facilitate this state.

The following aspects are important:

- Your posture: Enables a positive energy flow (sitting correctly, holding your back straight, holding your head and arms correctly)
- How you hold your sticks: Enables energy to flow through to the tips
- Your frame of mind: Take a relaxed approach, don't try to force anything
- Removing all obstacles: Allows natural, flowing movement
- Heightened senses: Perception of the space you're in, listening to the sound of your playing
- Careful, measured use of muscle power
- The correct drum setup: Especially for lefties, ensuring your drum set is configured to allow you to lead with your left hand/foot.

All of these factors play an essential role in helping you achieve the desired state. Your own actions need to take a backseat here! Paying too much attention to yourself and what you're doing can kill this precious phenomenon – making it even more difficult to hold onto the feeling of lightness and floating once it occurs. At the end of the day I see it as a gift: It can be bestowed upon you, but there's no guarantee it will be.

That said, you can achieve this once you learn, through experience, which "buttons you can push" to enable this state. That's the beauty of it!

Unfortunately, the door to this amazing natural high seems to remain closed, if not locked for left-handed drummers who play on right-handed drum sets – at least I've rarely heard of anyone in that situation who's ever experienced it. So please indulge me when I, once again, plead my case for left-handed drummers playing on a left-handed drum set.

15. YOUR SENSE OF PERCEPTION

Once you begin to experience this amazing "gift" more often, your sense of perception begins to change. This experience can manifest itself in many different dimensions, but here I'll focus on space and time – which is, after all, our core focus in drumming – we move our sticks through space and strike our beats at specific points in time.

Oddly enough, many drummers are only marginally aware of this space around them, if at all. And yet we make relatively large movements though that space, releasing acoustic vibrations which radiate out to our listeners. If we use space as a tool in our playing, we're able to achieve more precise timing. And when we assure that both the rise and fall of our drum sticks are smooth and steady, we are rewarded with a satisfying acoustic result.

The exact moment when the drumstick makes contact with the drumhead is extremely brief; it's difficult if not impossible for us to control. That said, the entire range of motion up to this point is very much within our sphere of control! If we start our upward motion earlier, our strike will come sooner. I can't tell you how often I've seen my students start their upward motion too late, and then try to make up for lost time by striking harder.

The same thing happens in our daily lives – who hasn't set off to an appointment too late, then tried to make up time by driving more quickly?

Whether we're playing an instrument or living our everyday lives, the same rules apply in both cases when it comes to how we interact with time. The progress we make with timing on our drum set is reflected in how we deal with time in other, non-music related situations. Our new perspective on time helps us eliminate stress from our daily lives: We no longer fight against time, but rather move in harmony with time.

As your feeling for time improves, it may feel like time has slowed down; you discover its natural flow, which you can ride like a wave. As a result, you feel as if you've actually gained time.

Here, too, it's important to nurture this "gift". Temptation to break out of this unique state and fall back into our old routines lurk around every corner. Sometimes, our peers may even try to shake us out of this condition. Maybe they resent what we have, or are jealous. Or maybe they are just trying to get their share.

16. THE PROCESS OF RELEARNING

How do you feel after reading the last two chapters? Maybe you recognize your left-handed students who don't seem to be able to reach that natural "high" when everything falls into place, or whose efforts to fall in with time don't seem to bear fruit. Or maybe you as a left-handed drummer are wondering how you can unlock these "gifts" for yourself?

I invite you to join me on the next part of the journey: Now that we've discussed energy, flow and groove – and the roles of our dominant and passive sides – it's time to address how to deal with the shortcomings which lefties face when playing on a right-handed drum set.

Starting over

For someone who has been playing the "wrong way around" for some time, going back to the beginning and re-learning can feel like an unsurmountable task. At the very least, it's something you instinctively shy away from.

The impulse to re-learn can only come from a drummer themselves – it's not something an instructor can or should try to force upon their students. Nor is it something which can be done "on the side" or be taken care of in a few simple lessons. Re-learning brings significant changes: Not only physical, but also emotional and maybe even health-related. Therefore, you can only be successful if you're driven by your own internal motivation.

How to best spark that motivation? By understanding what you can achieve; better yet, getting a feel for how different things could be. It's important to gather personal experience along the way to back up theoretical knowledge. This will help motivate you, confirming you're on the right path.

I, too, hesitated at first. But I finally agreed to take this step after my instructor shared his experience of how amazing it feels when you play the "other way around". Experiencing the first tiny sparks of success helped me finally comprehend what I stood to gain – my initial steps filled me with energy and helped turn the strenuous work into a positive challenge. The moment you feel that "wow, there's really something in this" – you're ready to commit and work even harder.

The re-learning process is an amazing journey. Full of ups and downs, it's not a journey to be embarked upon alone. It's critical that the instructor be willing to work closely with their student and accompany them over a longer time period – at least 2 to 3 months to start off with. More likely than not your student (you) will experience highs and lows which sow doubt about whether this was such a good idea after all; an instructor can provide guidance and moral support, helping keep you from throwing in the towel and quitting.

In the rest of this chapter I address two audiences: Instructors accompanying their left-handed students, and left-handed drummers themselves.

Interesting Discoveries

My own "a-ha moment" came the first time I felt the natural tension between the bass drum –now played with my left foot – and the snare drum now played with my right hand. You can imagine my instructor's reaction when he noticed this change in my next lesson: *"Finally! Now you know what I've been talking about all these years!"*

Even today, when I play the bass drum with my "wrong" (right) foot, I don't really feel anything. I hear the beat, get the timing right, can even play some pretty challenging stuff… but I don't really <u>feel</u> anything. On the other hand, when I play the same beat with my left foot, I feel a clear connection to my gut; I can truly play the beat following my "gut feel". This kind of personal experience is the strongest motivation to re-learn. Once you've experienced this powerful feeling yourself, you instinctively want more.

Let me share a few more inspiring stories from my experiences with students:

A 9-year old girl who had been taking lessons in a public music school for 2 years was re-assigned to me. In our first session I asked her if she was right or left-handed. She answered "left-handed" in a very self-assured manner, but then walked right past the left-handed drum set to sit at the one set up for right-handed students. I was perplexed, to say the least. She explained that her previous teacher told her it was important to learn to play on a right-handed set, because all drums were set up that way – it was the standard. She was absolutely adamant about not wanting to "start all over again"!

I wanted to make it as easy as possible for her, and was soon able to encourage her to sit at the left-handed set and give it a try. She carefully played a few beats on the bass drum with her left foot, then added the snare drum, then quickly built in the hi-hat accompaniment. Her first groove! She was positively beaming as it came so easily to her!

At her next lesson just a week later, she came running up to me with her mother calling behind her *"Mr. Bittner! Mr. Bittner! You have no idea what you've done! She won't stop practicing, she's having a ball... it's a real metamorphosis! Thank you!"*

A 25-year old student in a large respected drum school was a serial instructor-switcher; it didn't take long for him to be passed on from one to the next. His reputation – challenging to teach, to put it nicely – preceded him. After a colleague discovered he was left-handed, he was duly passed on to me.

This young man was very talented; he'd dedicated a lot of time to practicing and wanted to become a professional drummer. Naturally this made the decision whether or not to re-learn that much more difficult! But eventually, after long and careful preparation, we embarked together upon "Project Re-Learn".

Out first step was to seek that one killer beat, starting with the bass drum. His first taste of success came quickly; he felt a whole new energy through his left-foot bass beat in our very first session. It didn't take long for his snare drum to take on a whole new meaning. His "stuttering" playing style loosened and grew smoother, he improved his timing issues and the positive feedback from his band did the rest of the job.

This experience helped him discover a whole new sense of lightness. With every lesson he told me about new successes, such as how quickly he was able to learn new exercises. He was accomplishing much more with less practice time than before!

About two years on, he spoke to me about how not just his drumming, but his whole life had profited from this new sense of lightness. His studies at university improved – he was able to study more efficiently and his grades got better. His friends told him he was friendlier, easier to be around; simply "cooler". He hadn't realized how different things had been before.

He didn't become a professional drummer after all, but decided to go into engineering instead. He hasn't stopped drumming, though – and is really enjoying music and life.

A 12-year old student was really struggling with reading music. She struck me as a very musical, alert and creative young lady. She played in her local village band, where her director both supported and challenged her. Despite this, however, she was missing a sense of structure when it came to interpreting songs in the form of written music. As you can imagine, this was a source of ongoing conflict and stress.

Hers was a puzzling situation: Although she had a great sense of rhythm and showed real talent, once she sat down at the drum set and began to practice, her enthusiasm fizzled out. Despite my suspicions, she vehemently protested that she wasn't left-handed; she wrote with her right hand and had never even considered that she may be a lefty.

She continued to complain about the same struggles during every lesson, yet wasn't open to entertain the idea she may be left-handed. As you can imagine, it was becoming a tiresome situation for both of us!

After my patience had been stretched just about to the breaking point, my arguments finally fell on fertile ground. She agreed accept a bet and play left-handed for one week. Just to give it a try.

Guess what? In her very next lesson she asked to keep going – she had no desire to go back to playing right-handed! She had felt the bass drum more intensively, could remember grooves much more easily, and sat at the drum set with a genuine smile on her face.

A few lessons later, I placed some sheet music on her stand. It was like a curtain coming down – she immediately reverted to her former behavior and rejected the suggestion. I guess it shouldn't have come as a surprise; after all, her prior experiences with reading music had all been negative. Once again I carefully bartered with her, until she agreed to give it a try. And what do you know – she played the first few lines smoothly, without one mistake! She was somehow able to interpret the written music intuitively, without giving it too much thought. As you can expect, she was blown away by this experience and couldn't believe what she'd been able to do. For me, that was the final "proof" that she was, indeed, a lefty. This was all she needed to convince her to stay on her new left-handed path. Her newly found orientation spread beyond just music – she sought other things in life she could "switch" to left, too. She even went to battle with her music teacher at school, who stuck with his mantra that drums simply must be played "right".

Total Motivation

As I mentioned earlier, a key to success is personally experiencing advantages which were, up to this point, theoretical. I call these discoveries, and would like to share three important ones with you now. If you're an instructor, help prepare your students for these discoveries, and give them lots of reinforcement when they happen. And if you're a lefty considering embarking on this journey yourself, keep your eyes out for these milestones.

Probably the most powerful discovery of all is experiencing a new kind of energy. The first time you no longer simply play the "1" (downbeat) on the bass drum but feel it resonate deep inside of you; when it gives you an intense feeling of being "grounded" and feels like a powerful stomp on the ground; then, and only then, have you internalized the true role of the bass drum beat. The snare drum, in turn, no longer feels like something you blindly pound with your leading hand, but sets an upbeat which complements the strong beat provided by the bass drum. This counterpart is graced with a special sense of lightness, as it's taken over by our "naïve" non-dominant right hand.

This intuitive gut feel for the downbeat and upbeat leads to nothing less than epiphany for any left-handed drummer. Finally, you experience the (formerly elusive) polarity everyone has been talking about! This is powerful stuff... once you feel this new energy, you can't get enough – it's an incredible motivation to keep going!

Here's a metaphor for you: Imagine sitting in a sports car and stepping on the gas. Unleashing 300 horsepower will pin just about anyone into their seat! The energy you unleash when playing the drums, in contrast, feels much more subtle, but grows incredibly strong once activated. The energy I get from drumming has a stronger impact on me personally, as it's complemented by a mysterious element, something almost supernatural; something we can't really put our finger on. Honestly, the fastest sports car in the world can't begin to compete with it!

The second discovery we make when re-learning, which also gives us a huge motivation boost, is how easy reading music becomes. Lefties who play on a right-handed drum set don't intuitively feel the first strong downbeat in each new measure. This makes it difficult to orient ourselves in written music, which appears as an endless stream of notes and rests, often without rhyme or reason. It's no wonder we tend to get lost! That's why it's critically important to ensure you clearly feel the first strong downbeat – the "1" – in each new measure. Every other note stands in relation to the "1" – for example, the second beat only makes sense in context with the first.

It's important to take this part slowly, taking the time to build a deep understanding of the relation of each beat to the others. For example, in 4/4 time: The "2" can only take on its proper role if the "1" is played confidently. Then we continue in turn with the "3" and the "4"; then come the eighth notes "1-and-2-and"… and so on. Once we internalize this, reading music is no longer an image-recognition exercise, but rather a process of recalling familiar patterns and motions – the basis for making music. Because as long as we burn up time and energy with the technical deciphering of written notes, we aren't free to interpret the music we set out to play!

Let me stress again how important it is in this first phase to take things slowly and go back to the basics. Allow yourself time to master basic note patterns and beats before tackling faster, more complex passages. This can really try your patience, especially if you were an advanced drummer before re-learning. But believe me – going too quickly can unravel all your hard work! Don't put yourself under pressure; slowly and gradually increase the level of difficulty. Tackling several lines of a song won't help you reach your goal more quickly – it's more effective to take just a few measures at a time and repeat them frequently. Trust me – less is more!

As a left-handed drummer begins to get a sense of orientation, you recognize how easy reading music can actually be – no need for an instructor to keep making this point. Once the proverbial switch is thrown and you can easily sight-read passages without making mistakes, it's OK to move on and tackle more advanced material.

The third, probably most motivating discovery is how much more effective your practice sessions become. Most lefties playing on a right-handed drum set have to sink a lot of time and repetition into learning something new. Imagine your delight once you notice how you master new sequences played "the other way around" much more quickly! Where you once needed ten repetitions, you now only need a couple. You recognize how different elements are related to one another with ease, and execute them more effectively.

I personally experienced a great leap in efficiency: It used to be a daunting, if not impossible task to learn a page of new grooves within a week. After switching, I intuitively recognize similarities between grooves, and can effectively implement what I've already learned when tackling new figures further down the page. I see it in my students, too – their practice sessions gain a whole new structure and purpose.

It doesn't take long and the instructor will recognize how their student's personal playing style begins to emerge. In these early stages, though, the student themselves probably won't notice – so it's important that instructors reinforce these first positive changes!

Others will likely notice your progress, too. Stay open for feedback, and don't be surprised when you get positive reactions from other band members. If you play concerts, you may get praise from people in the audience; family, friends, boyfriends and girlfriends are all likely to comment on the big difference they've heard. This is the point when lefties get the ultimate validation that re-learning was the right decision: Hurdles have been torn down, nothing stands in the way! Whether it's the love of music or the fascination for movement or rhythm; you've finally come into your own.

Most left-handed drummers hesitate before deciding to embark on the process of re-learning. By this point, at the very latest, any final remaining doubts or hesitation are removed; the choice feels like it was inevitable. Memories of prior struggles start to fade. It's fascinating how quickly we can forget the negative once things start going well.

It's a real shame that there are still left-handed drummers out there who continue to stumble in the dark. Therefore I appeal to each and every one of you who has gone through this process personally or accompanied a student: Please, spread the word! Talk about it, share your experiences with others. Here's hoping your anecdotes will fall on fertile ground.

Hitting rock bottom; flipping the switch in your brain

If all of this sounds too good to be true and you're wondering why I warned of the challenges accompanying re-learning; well, now comes the hard part. Once we experience our first "highs" and newly found motivation is coursing through our veins… comes our first crash. Our elation is replaced by a sense of crisis. Sure, we've made great progress and gotten a taste of how much better we can play. But we set the bar too high, and are bitterly disappointed when our actual achievements fall short of our expectations.

To make matters worse, we realize that we no longer play as well on the right-handed drum set as we did before switching. Yet we still have a way to go before reaching our former level on the new left-handed drum set. It feels like being stuck in the middle of a long tunnel: We've come too far to turn back, but are a long way from reaching the other end. Feeling that both ends of the tunnel are just beyond our reach can plunge us into frustration, leading us to doubt once again if we did the right thing. We may even consider throwing in the towel and quitting.

What triggers this crisis? I've experienced this phenomenon in another context, so join me as I take a detour from playing the drums to learning a foreign language.

During the 1980's I left Germany for a year to live in the United States. My English was pretty good before I moved; but after about three months I hit a wall. It felt like I couldn't speak English anymore, and even listening to English gave me a headache. More strangely, it felt like I'd lost my command of German, too! Trying to speak or even think in German made me feel like my head was going to explode. I just wanted to get away – either return home, or go anywhere but where I was.

Two years later, a friend I made during that time came to live in Germany. Originally from Ireland, he struggled to find work there and decided to try his luck in Bavaria, where his field was booming. He didn't speak a word of German when he arrived. Thanks to studying hard – and with the help of his new friends, newspapers, and television – he picked up a fair amount of German pretty quickly. That said, he was still thinking in English and translating. Oddly enough, after some time he hit the same wall that

I did: German made his head spin, he couldn't stand it anymore – he wanted to go back to Ireland. But – just like me – his native language also tied his tongue and brain in knots!

I think this phenomenon happens when our brains re-wire. During my own language crisis I woke up one morning realizing that I had dreamt in English; from that point on, I started to think in English, too. My American and Irish friends got a real kick out of me telling jokes in English! As you probably expected, the same thing happened to my Irish friend here. We were able to convince him to stay and ride it out; he did, with success. He started thinking in German, then found himself struggling to find words in English. His brain had successfully thrown the switch to living and thinking in German – including telling German jokes!

I've witnessed similar experiences in left-handed drum students I've accompanied as they re-learn. After hitting rock-bottom, they emerged from their crises stronger than ever, their brains settling into the new "normal". The process of re-learning had effectively re-wired their brains, enabling them to intuitively act according to their natural impulses.

It's important to go into the process of re-learning with your eyes open, knowing that this crisis will strike at some point. But you, too, will emerge stronger on the other side. Knowing what will happen, and understanding that it's a critical part of the process can help you get through this dark period, giving you the strength and courage to keep going. Another reason not to head into this alone – but to have a guide you trust at your side. This process takes time; it will probably take you longer to emerge from the tunnel than you would like.

The role of the Guide

I've gone through the re-learning process myself, and have also shared the experience with several students. Still, each time I accompany a new student on their re-learning journey it's a real challenge not just for them, but for me, too. It's not easy for the instructor to take control and help the student see the light at the end of the tunnel. It takes a lot of time and patience! But it doesn't come without its reward: Together, you are sure to reach your goal. Due to the very nature of the process, how could it be any different?

Although too much pressure can do more harm than good, it helps if you convey a certain sense of obligation or sense of personal responsibility to your student. They recognize your experience as an instructor, which helps win their trust. Parallel to that, you also place your trust in your student, and in their ability to learn. In this sense, your student wants to fulfill your expectations and pay you – the instructor – back for your trust. Use this to help keep them on track, so they don't give in to temptation and quit when things get rough. The temptation to give up would be even stronger if it wasn't for your guiding presence – unfortunately, the student's own self-confidence often isn't enough.

I'm sad to say I've had a student quit in the middle of their "stuck in the tunnel" crisis, as his doubts outweighed his positive experiences until that point. Let me share this bitter experience with you, so you can share in what I learned. Looking back, I now recognize that a key mistake was leaving too much time between lessons. He lived relatively far away from the school, and spaced his lessons every 2 to 4 weeks. I distinctly remember a powerful lesson filled with emotion – I was really thrilled to see the seed of enthusiasm starting to take root. Imagine my disappointment when, two weeks later, he cancelled his next lesson; two weeks following that, he cancelled his lessons with me completely. I've since learned that he went back to playing on a right-handed drum set, and continues to struggle.

What can we learn from this? My experience shows that students do best with frequent lessons in which their instructor/guide exerts firm yet comfortable pressure. Students should feel a kind of obligation to deliver on the tasks they are given; consequently the instructor needs to have high degree of empathy and respect to know how much pressure is enough, yet not too much. Don't let too much space or time creep in between you — be sure to keep meeting for lessons on a regular basis!

When the effort pays off...

Let's fast-forward to the first positive phase: The student begins to notice the difference themselves. They recognize that the struggle, which is already beginning to fade from memory, was worth it. Everything feels right — how the body feels while playing, improved orientation, a new sense of lightness, how easy it has become to read music. Although they may not see it themselves, your student's face while playing has changed: Their strained expression has probably relaxed and been replaced by a smile. The hard work required to make progress has become less of a chore, practicing has finally become fun!

Even after our brains have flipped the switch we still occasionally mix things up, for example reacting with the wrong foot and striking the hi-hat instead of the bass drum. Don't forget — the new roles we've assigned our hands and feet need time before they are completely internalized. But don't worry, these incidents will happen less and less often, until they're a thing of the past.

You may sometimes feel like a complete beginner sitting down at a drum set for the first time. But don't be fooled, you're already a huge step ahead – everything you learned on the right-handed drum set is still there. You don't need to learn all over again, but simply adjust what you know to your new left-handed setup. This re-learning goes faster than you'd think; in any case faster than learning the first time around!

This new feeling while playing is just the beginning. But don't sell yourself short just yet! From the student's perspective, these new accomplishments feel intense and very rewarding. That's why it's so important for the instructor to keep pushing – gently yet firmly. It would be a shame for the student to stop now, satisfied with this first success, when there is so much more to be gained.

At this stage, our focus should be on further solidifying and internalizing what we've learned, through lots of practice and repetition. The stronger a foundation we can build, the more stable our house will stand. Keep in mind that the student may not yet not realize their full potential. With their newly found skills they'll be able to achieve things which seemed beyond reach, and attain goals they never would have dreamed possible.

Baby steps

Please remember – as an instructor, it's crucial that you raise the bar very slowly and carefully. Beware getting caught up in the rush of success and racing off too quickly! The student will be able to quickly repeat new movements on demand. But don't be fooled – even though they successfully execute once doesn't mean they have committed something to muscle memory. Slow down, play around with newly acquired skills before moving on to the next step. Don't forget to do a quick check: Are they able to confidently execute – several times – without any hesitation or undue effort? Only after you're sure they've truly mastered a new skill is it time to take the next step.

Why this cautious approach? It takes time for the brain to "re-wire". During this process, your student may feel like a boat being tossed about in a storm on high seas; they are likely to crave a "safe harbor" where they feel protected and secure. Proceeding too quickly can lead to a new sense of disorientation; in the worst case, the student may question this new way of playing and be tempted to throw in the towel. Give them the chance to slowly but surely build up their confidence in this new method. Forgive me for repeating myself, but I can't say it enough: Less is more!

Remember when I compared the incredible sense of energy you can get from drumming to a kind of drug-induced "high"? Imagine what it must be like for your student when they get their first real taste – it will unlock a new drive and yearning for more. So don't be surprised when they come begging for another "hit" – in the form of more complex material. My advice to you at this point: Stand your ground. Be firm, reinforce their accomplishments but keep them on an even keel. Cautiously rein them back in by giving them new skills to practice steadily, one after the other.

Sustainable development is best achieved through small but effective steps. It's not unlike mountain climbing – steady progress is difficult if individual steps are too large. Each "leap" requires too much energy and you lack a methodical approach to covering distance. Best case is the student discovers this themselves, and recognizes the improvement which each little step brings. A good instructor will give the student enough room to make this discovery – helping prepare the trail by keeping an eye out for and removing any hurdles.

Playing the hi-hat with your right foot

Let's fast-forward to an important skill you'll need to (re) learn: Playing the hi-hat with your right foot. In case you're skipping ahead, hang on... You're ready for this step once you're confident leading with your left hand during fills played with the tom-toms, as well as grooves with the hi-hat, bass drum and snare drum. And, most essentially, you should be able to confidently play the bass drum with your left foot – even in your sleep! Not quite there yet? Put in some more practice first; don't worry, this next step will be waiting for you when you come back.

It's tricky because up until now, our left foot played the hi-hat; its new role on the bass drum is the complete opposite! So don't be surprised that when you first play the hi-hat with your right foot, all kinds of old memories will be re-activated and you're likely to mix up the roles of your two feet; you'll play bass drum beats with the hi-hat and vice-versa. But don't panic – dedicate some time to careful practice and you'll get the hang of it.

Ready? Here are some exercises which have proven to be effective helping students get a good feel for the new roles of their right and left feet. The following five steps are sequential; for best results, dedicate time – about two weeks of dedicated practice – to really master each step before moving on to the next.

Step 1: Play the hi-hat with your foot on 2 and 4

We'll use the same basic setup for all five steps: Left hand on the ride cymbal, right hand on the snare; left foot on the bass drum and right foot on the hi-hat.

Play an easy pattern, such as eighth notes, with your left hand on the ride cymbal. Strike the hi-hat with your right foot on the back beat, in synch with the snare drum. The left foot plays an intensive "1" (downbeat) on the bass drum, and the right foot channels the energy of the back beat played on the snare drum.

Step 2: Only play with your feet

Keep going with the same easy groove from Step 1 – but only play with your feet, using the bass drum and hi-hat. Here, you should focus on feeling the different energy flows coming from each of your feet as you play. Work on getting a strong downbeat with your left foot and putting some sass into your upbeat with your right foot. See if you can't get a real groove going with your feet!

Step 3: Adding your hands

Once you've got an intensive groove going with your feet, it's time to bring your hands back into play. Don't over-think it; play anything that comes to mind with your hands. If you're not comfortable improvising, then pick out a rhythmic phrase you'd like to play. I recommend doing this exercise on practice pads, which will help keep you focused on the motions you're making rather than the sound you're creating.

As soon as you hands start to play, your feet will probably fade into the background. Your goal here is to really internalize what you're doing with your feet – don't let your hands distract you and steal the show! Pull your attention away from your hands, keeping your full focus on the new roles your feet are learning.

Step 4: Play a groove with and without the hi-hat

Start this step without the hi-hat. Play a groove with your left hand on the ride cymbal and throw yourself into it – let your emotions take over until you lose yourself in an intensive groove! It's important to really give it all you've got.

Then – add the hi-hat (played with your right foot) to the backbeat, in synch with the snare drum. Can you maintain the intensity of your groove? Our goal here is that the hi-hat, played with your foot, doesn't get in the way of the rest of your motions. The hi-hat is only an accompaniment, adding a slight nuance to your groove.

Step 5: Play a groove with a variation on the hi-hat

Once the prior 4 steps have been mastered, it's time to move on to accompanying grooves with the hi-hat, played with our right foot, on the quarters or "and" beats. I recommend starting off playing quarters with the hi-hat. Once you are able to hold a very steady rhythm, slowly add in the ride cymbal, snare drum and bass drum – one at a time. If your hi-hat remains steady, you can try adding in a complete groove.

The danger to watch out for is that your right foot, now playing the hi-hat, will "remember" its former role on the bass drum and start to take the lead in the groove. To help keep this from happening, it's important to play a really dominant bass drum with your left foot, so that each foot can internalize its new role.

Playing the hi-hat on the "and" (every second eighth-note) can be very helpful in further solidifying the role of each foot. But don't be surprised – this exercise is technically demanding! The hi-hat should stay fresh, even "sassy" as it drives the groove ahead. For this to work, the bass drum needs to be even more "grounded", and should come just a touch too late.

This exercise can serve as a good self-test to see to what extent our energy has been correctly re-assigned to each foot; has each confidently adopted its new role? If we still have too many artifacts from playing the "wrong" way around in our system, it's incredibly hard to keep a groove steady while playing the hi-hat with our right foot: Our feet will keep getting mixed up. If you notice this happening, don't despair – go back and work on each of the first 4 steps again, taking your time to truly commit each step to muscle memory. You'll get there!

17. OUR FEMININE AND MASCULINE SIDES

Earlier on I spoke about the differences between our left-brain and right-brain, as well as polarity. Now that we've discussed the process of re-learning to play the drums left-handed, I'd like to take another look at differences between the two sides of our bodies which you may well notice in your drumming.

Each side of our body has its own attributes: Our right side carries more masculine, our left side feminine characteristics. This doesn't have anything to do with our gender, or being a man or a woman! These two opposite poles can be found in each of us. While some of us tend to display masculine characteristics more strongly, others express more feminine ones.

What do I mean by masculine and feminine? Typical masculine attributes are: Impulsive, external and forward-facing, militant, dynamic, performance-oriented, competitive, destructive, active. On the other hand, typical feminine attributes are: Demonstrative, diffuse, ebbing, emotional, lacking clear form, constructive, creative, fruitful, receiving, healing, devoted, passive. (These lists are by no means complete; there is a wealth of sources you can check out if you'd like to learn more on this topic!)

I have yet to meet a left-handed person whose masculine characteristics outweigh the feminine. Instead, all the lefties I know tend to express feminine traits more strongly. That leads me to wonder if the left side of our bodies tends to carry more feminine traits, or if my observation is simply random in nature.

I've also noticed that beginner and early intermediate male drummers tend to have more power in their playing than their left-handed counterparts. Lefties, in comparison, tend to play somewhat softer and lighter. I've also noticed this same reserved, soft playing style in right-handed women, whereby left-handed female drummers tend to play with a lot more power. In advanced drummers, though, these differences tend to balance each other out until, over time, they are no longer noticeable.

I'm not 100% sure, but suspect this is a direct effect of how much attention we pay to our bodies' energy flow while we play. Over time, we drummers dedicate a lot of effort to loosening up and exercising our more passive side. This enables our natural polarity to fully develop until both poles are equally strong and hold each other in balance. This leaves no noticeable difference in power between advanced right-handed and left-handed drummers of either gender. However, a difference in the impact of their playing style does remain. Let me explain that further in the next chapter.

18. ALLOCATION OF THE POLES

Numerous sources allocate the plus pole (masculine attributes) to the right side of our bodies, and the minus pole (feminine attributes) to our left sides – for right-handed people. How these poles are allocated in left-handed people, though, is seldom discussed. It seems to be taken for granted that lefties are exact opposites of righties – which would mean that our plus pole is allocated to our leading, or left side. But I'm not so sure about that anymore. A few things have led me to believe that the allocation of the poles is the same for all of us: The plus pole is attributed to the right side for lefties, too.

I started to question this after reading a spiritual article about the laying of hands which explained the importance of which hand you use: The left hand absorbs energy, and is the minus pole. The right hand gives energy and is the plus pole – and this also holds true for left-handed people! This came as a surprise to me; I thought if lefties wanted to give energy, they would probably instinctively use their left hand.

Considering this new perspective, it no longer comes as a surprise that I've always sensed a completely different kind of energy when left-handed drummers play a groove. Lefties strike the snare drum with their right hand – the "plus" pole. This leads the energy in the groove to radiate outwards – in contrast to right-handed drummers whose snare-drum strikes are inwardly focused. So it's no wonder that from an early age I've been fascinated by Ian Paice, the left-handed drummer of Deep Purple. More than anything it's the expression in his snare drum which really enthralls me. A couple of years later another left-handed drummer captivated me with a similar fascination – none other than Phil Collins.

Please don't misunderstand me, I'm not placing any kind of judgement here, nor am I suggesting that either way of playing is "better" than the other. It's simply my personal perception that the plus-pole energy of the right hand releases the unique potential of the snare drum: Fresh, lively and with a strong forward drive. Add the left foot on the bass drum to this mix, with the feminine characteristics of being grounded, earthy and material; for me, this energy is a perfect complement to a rich "1" in the bass drum.

If we look at it this way, the drum set is an instrument which perfectly fits our natural disposition as lefties. We generate a completely different kind of energy than right-handed drummers – something we should cultivate in our playing and make the most of!

19. OPEN-HANDED DRUMMING

I've been coming across more and more drummers recently who speak out in favor of open-handed drumming. Even some well-known instructors and coaches actively promote this style of playing. This technique certainly presents a challenge which appeals to some drummers; for me, it's more akin to practicing a sport than following your inner drive to make music.

There are many highly talented and successful drummers these days – the competition is immense. Some seek new fields where they can differentiate themselves from the crowd by claiming a sort of niche in the market. In my opinion, following the open-handed path leads to a dead-end.

I can't help but wonder: What led people who first "invented" and set up a drum set to then play with crossed hands? These pioneering drummers probably weren't highly intellectual theorists, driven by their heads more than their hearts. They were doubtless very in tune with their bodies and gifted with great coordination, driven by an inner impulse to play with their hands crossed.

Vinnie Colaiuta, a highly talented drummer who's worked as a studio musician across a wide range of genres and has accompanied many famous acts, gave a workshop at Drummers Focus in Munich in 1995. He was way ahead of his time when answering a question from the audience about open-handed playing, taking a very clear stance on the issue: "*Why*", he said very slowly, emphasizing each word, *"the fuck should I ever do this?"*

Open-handed drumming doesn't allow a natural groove to develop, because polarity and a natural field of tension are missing; the bass drum and snare drum are both played with the same side of the body. Even if you place every strike correctly and perfect your timing, the natural energy flow just won't be there.

Some open-hand drummers have previously played with crossed hands, thereby experiencing a true groove. This helps them re-create a feeling of groove when playing open-handed. But no matter how gifted they play, it remains a copy of their natural drumming instinct. I've noticed how some of these drummers develop an intense groove as soon as they play the ride-cymbal. With their right hand on the ride-cymbal, left hand on the snare drum and right foot on the bass drum they reach a constellation which sets their natural energy field free. But as soon as they switch their left hand to the hi-hat and play open-handed, that energy evaporates – even though their playing remains acoustically correct, something essential is missing.

Of course everyone is free to look into and experiment with this technique; many proponents of open-handed drumming argue their case by naming several advantages it can bring. For me, though, these are outweighed by the potential drawbacks.

Here's how I see it:
There are some very advanced drummers out there who make open-handed drumming look highly compelling. But watch out: There's a huge difference between an advanced drummer with strong experience in independence, groove and energy taking on a new challenge and a beginner or amateur drummer. For the latter, this same

challenge could end up leading down a path which hinders rather than helps development.

20. LEFT-HANDED & RIGHT-FOOTED

Over the years I've encountered drummers who see themselves as left-handed and right-footed, or the other way around. My experience has led me to believe that each and every one of us has one naturally dominant side, either right or left. So what to make of these "mixed" people?

I once had the opportunity to work with a student who claimed to be left-handed, as he wrote with his left hand. That said, he did everything else with this right hand. He even saw himself as right-footed. When he played on a right-handed drum set, though, his playing was so rich in energy that I had to convince him – against much protesting – to abandon his plans to re-learn on a left-handed set!

Significant life events in our early years can leave powerful impressions, sometimes meaningful enough to lead a naturally right-handed person to do things with their left hand. For example, a left-handed role model could make such a strong impression on a child that they subconsciously imitate their left-handedness. In addition to psychological drivers, health issues could also lead someone to switch from their initial disposition. A young student's mother once told me how he had suffered a slight brain hemorrhage earlier in his childhood; since then, he hadn't displayed any clear signs of being either right or left handed.

For some of us, though, it's not so easy to tell. One of my students asked me in our very first lesson if I thought he was left or right handed. Although he was pretty sure he was left-handed, he assumed he was right footed, as he was totally unable to kick a ball with his left foot. After playing a few exercises with him on the drum set it was as clear as could be – he should be playing left-handed! His left foot had so much more power and expression on the bass drum than his right. Although he didn't perceive the difference himself, anyone listening could clearly hear how the combination of his left foot on the bass drum and right hand on the snare was full of positive energy and just felt right – as opposed to his right foot on the bass drum and left hand on snare, which felt dull and empty.

I shared this experience with another student who also has far better ball control with his right than with his left foot. In his case, though, he rejected playing the bass drum with his "strong" right foot, as earlier attempts to do so didn't feel right. Interesting to note is that this student has been a confident left-hander since early childhood, and has since become a semi-professional drummer!

Bear with me as I share one more example: Several years ago, a 12-year old student began lessons with me convinced he was left-handed and right-footed. His strong self-assuredness led me to accept this, so we proceeded with his lessons accordingly. That said, I still tried from time to time to persuade him to dedicate himself completely to one side or the other; just try out how it feels to play as a true left or right-hander.

Well, a few years later he came into his lesson grinning from ear to ear. He'd tried an experiment and switched to play the hi-hat with his right hand! In doing so, he discovered a kind of energy and flow in his playing he'd never experienced before. As I listened, I was totally taken aback by the new expression in his play. Despite knowing him for years, this simple change had unlocked a whole new dimension I'd never heard! From this point on he's been playing right-handed, and has decided to become a professional drummer – something he's well on his way to achieving.

Many of these kinds of experiences have convinced me that what we believe to be our strong hand or foot isn't always the same as our naturally dominant side; this "strength" is something we may consciously or unconsciously acquire during childhood in our use of certain toys, tools or other activities. The natural dominance we have on one side of our bodies can, but isn't always linked with muscular strength.

21. CLOSING COMMENTS: NOW WHAT?

As I sat down to write this book, I did a lot of reading and a great deal of reflecting. First of all on my own experiences, then what I'd seen and heard from others. While some of what I learned came as a surprise, many things confirmed and explained what I had already suspected, felt or gone through myself.

I'm increasingly fascinated by energy and polarity. Although these topics often tend towards the esoteric, it naturally makes sense to me that these forces play a main role not just in which hand takes the lead when we play the drums, but how we approach, organize and carry out many other tasks in life. I can't help but think that if we dedicate more time to being open to and exploring these forces in our own bodies, it can only have a positive impact. Regardless of whether we lead with our left or right hand, regardless of how we set up our drum sets, if we experiment with different combinations and act on what we feel as a result, our drumming can only get better.

If readers take one thing out of my book, I hope it's this: Don't give up! Keep going – you'll make it! I have a special wish for all you lefties: Be open to discovering the feeling of lightness! It's real, and you, too, can experience it.

Music serves as a kind of language; a language of truth which knows no lies. For us to be able to communicate with music in a true and natural way, I encourage us all to adopt a true and natural attitude towards life and towards ourselves.

Many of us seek some kind of instrument to help us develop personally and find our way in life, have fun, re-energize, overcome adversity, heal, solve problems or simply to occupy our time.

Why not a musical instrument?

MY STORY:
HOW RELEARNING CHANGED MY LIFE

I was born in January 1966 in Munich, Germany. My childhood was very happy, as I grew up in a loving family with my mother, father and younger brother. We were fortunate, and didn't want for anything.

My first "official" contact with music came when I was six and started piano lessons. Reading music was extremely difficult for me, as I had to decipher every single note, thinking "when I see this symbol, I have to press this key". I got around this by learning everything by heart – pretending that I was reading the music as I played. Four long years later, after many tears and much drama, the dreaded piano lessons finally came to an end. As an alternative, my mother suggested "jazz piano". Now that was something I liked!

In the two years that followed I instinctively learned a lot about relationships in music – why some things sounded good, while others didn't. Rather than learning written songs, I improvised and made up my own pieces. That was a lot more enjoyable, and I still profit from what I learned back then! I often played challenging runs in bass tones with my left hand, accompanied by simple chords with my right hand. In retrospect this is no surprise; even then, on the piano, I was leading with my left hand.

When I was 11 years old, I started drumming along with music on the radio. Using drumsticks I carved out of firewood, I'd sit on my bed "drumming" on different colored cushions. But that wasn't good enough, so I quickly graduated to "drums" created out of empty laundry detergent boxes. I played along to the radio for hours, tapping the beats I heard; this gave me a solid grounding in typical 70's music.

The first true milestone in my life was my first decent drum set: A TAMA Royal Star with Paiste cymbals. There was no question how to set up my new drums. I'd never seen anything other than the "standard" setup for right-handed drummers, so naturally I set mine up that way too, following all the pictures I'd ever seen. Self-taught, I didn't have an instructor to suggest there could be a different way of doing things.

From that point on, I practiced a lot. Wearing headphones, I filtered grooves, fills and breaks out of the music myself. It was all intuition, I wasn't following any particular method, and my "lessons" didn't have any structure. In the years that followed, I played with many different bands. I'd earned the reputation of being a "musical" drummer; not someone who hammers out grooves that the rest of the band is damned to follow, but who listens and fits in with what the rest of the band is doing.

With my first job came my own income; I could finally pay for drum lessons at the recommended "Dante Agostini Schlagzeugschule" (drum school) in Munich. At this stage, my instructor remarked that I was doing pretty well; he never criticized my self-taught "open hand" drumming. Although I had a few issues executing certain patterns designed for right-handed drummers, everything was going pretty much OK. That said, I still had serious problems reading music, just as when I was a child playing the piano. So I continued to invest a great deal of effort in memorizing songs.

When I was 22 my dream of becoming a professional drummer took me abroad. A friend of mine was already living in Boston, so I had a place to crash. Berklee College of Music not only accepted my application but awarded me an international scholarship, cementing my choice.

When I returned home to Munich a year later I was really looking forward to continuing my studies at the Munich drum school, which had been renamed "Drummer's Focus". I felt very much in my element there, and received private lessons which were pretty intensive and had a great deal of depth and substance. Although my instructors weren't always gentle as they trained me to be a professional drummer, this approach was more in harmony with my German mindset.

Ironically, switching to instructor Cloy Peterson, founder and head of Drummer's Focus, plunged me into the deepest crisis I'd experienced as a drummer. After making slow but steady improvements I'd become stuck, simply treading water instead of making progress. As my fellow band members continued to develop, so too did their expectations. They gently but honestly gave me feedback that my playing wasn't rich enough, I was missing essential energy and groove.

Although Cloy displayed all the patience in the world, it became clear that if I kept things as-is, I wasn't going to be able to meet his expectations. He never pushed me, but also never tired of suggesting I try to switch my drum set around and play left-handed.

To make matters worse, I attempted but wasn't able to pass the next level of drum exams. I finally realized that I had to make a choice. If I wanted to reach my dream of becoming a professional drummer, I needed to follow Cloy's advice and re-learn the other way around. Which, at that point in time, felt like being condemned to start all over again. Tears were shed, but I recognized this was the only choice I could make.

Fast-forward two short years: I had not only caught up to where I was before, but actually passed myself; I could finally play things which used to be out of my reach. Even more, my struggles to read music were a thing of the past. I was really grooving. New doors were opening for me professionally – I was finally getting the kinds of offers I had been hoping for. It looked like I would actually be able to make a living with drumming. Another dream came true when Cloy asked me if I was interested in training as an instructor.

The following years were filled with practice and study, as my whole outlook on life, the world and the people in it changed. People have always fascinated me – one of the reasons I studied political science part-time at the Bavarian School of Public Policy in Munich. But after completing my Bachelor I realized there just weren´t enough hours the day for me to pursue all of my interests; it was time to make a choice between finishing my studies to earn my Master, or continue seriously with music. I made the commitment to focus on music.

In 2003 I dared to face my final personal hurdle and re-sat the exams marking the point where I had formerly gotten stuck. Well… this time around I passed with flying colors, which qualified me as a professional drummer. Four years later, I passed the final exams at the end of my teacher training courses to obtain my qualification as instructor.

From my current perspective as an instructor, I'm thankful for my slow and laborious learning process (during the years I played the "wrong" way around, on a right-handed drum set). The deep frustration I felt back then helps me empathize with my current students. I often see "little Thomas" sitting in front of me during lessons, and can totally relate to how my student feels and where they've gotten stuck. From where I sit now, it feels like my former weakness has become a strength.

Working as an instructor at Drummer's Focus in Munich has rewarded me with many rich experiences, which planted the seed in my mind to write this book.

THANKS

My warmest thanks to my loved ones who have supported and accompanied me along my way. But I also want to thank those who have provoked me, caused me problems, or even infuriated me. That, too, has helped me grow.

A special mention and thanks to the following people:

My wife Heike, for the incredible way she supports me, spurs me on, loves me, and always seems to know the right thing to say and do.

My instructor and mentor, Cloy Peterson, who showed so much patience with me, and opened up a whole new life to me. Thank you, Cloy, for creating the unique drum school "Drummer's Focus", and for guiding it through rough waters with your steady hand.

My close friends and fellow musicians who I have been making music (and growing) with almost all my life: Michael Benker, Robert Kopetz, Micha Voigt and Carsten Paul, to name a few.

My parents, who blessed me with a happy and carefree childhood in a loving family; giving me the strength to make my own way in life and never stop growing.

Elizabeth Lamberts, for translating my book into English with such dedication and enthusiasm.

Markus Unterthurner and Urban Piazzi from "updrums", whose amazing wooden snare drum I so enjoy playing. It can be seen on the cover page.

And finally, many thanks to Paiste. I've been a huge fan of the sound of their cymbals – 100% "my" sound – since my youth. I'm very grateful for the company's generous support, above all from Christian Wenzel.

www.ingramcontent.com/pod-product-compliance
Lightning Source LLC
Chambersburg PA
CBHW060806110426
42739CB00032BA/3120